The Story of
Anne Frank

by Rachel A. Koestler-Grack

CHELSEA
CLUBHOUSE

An Imprint of Chelsea House Publishers

A Haights Cross Communications Company

Philadelphia

Chelsea Clubhouse books are published by Chelsea House Publishers, a subsidiary of Haights Cross Communications

A Haights Cross Communications ✦ Company

The Chelsea House World Wide Web address is www.chelseahouse.com

Printed and bound in the United States of America.

9 8 7 6 5 4 3 2 1

Library of Congress Cataloging-in-Publication Data
Koestler-Grack, Rachel A., 1973–
  The story of Anne Frank / by Rachel A. Koestler-Grack.
      p. cm. — (Breakthrough biographies)
Summary: Discusses the life of Anne Frank and her family, who hid from soldiers in Nazi-occupied Holland for over two years by staying in a secret annex. Includes brief quotations from her diary.
Includes bibliographical references and index.
  ISBN 0-7910-7311-4
  1. Frank, Anne, 1929–1945—Juvenile literature. 2. Jewish children in the Holocaust—Netherlands—Amsterdam—Biography—Juvenile literature. 3. Jews—Netherlands—Amsterdam—Biography—Juvenile literature.
4. Amsterdam (Netherlands)—Biography—Juvenile literature. [1. Frank, Anne, 1929–1945. 2. Jews—Netherlands—Biography. 3. Holocaust, Jewish (1939–1945)—Netherlands—Amsterdam. 4. Women—Biography.] I. Title. II. Series.
  DS135.N6F73375 2004
  940.53'18'092—dc21   2003000266

Quotation Sources:
Anne Frank's quotations originate from:
Anne Frank: The Diary of a Young Girl (The Definitive Edition), edited by Otto H. Frank and Mirjam Pressler. New York: Doubleday, 1995.

Anne Frank's quotation on p. 17 is from:
Anne Frank, Beyond the Diary: A Photographic Remembrance, by Ruud van der Rol and Rian Verhoeven. New York: Viking, 1993.

Hannah Pick-Goslar is quoted from:
The Last Seven Months of Anne Frank, by Willy Lindwer. New York: Pantheon Books, 1991.

Editorial Credits
Colleen Sexton, editor; Takeshi Takahashi, designer; Mary Englar, photo researcher; Jennifer Krassy Peiler, layout

Content Reviewer
Stephen Feinstein, Director, Center for Holocaust and Genocide Studies, University of Minnesota

Photo Credits
©Hulton Archive/Getty Images: cover, title page, 5, 6, 7, 8, 12 (both), 14, 15, 17 (all), 18; ©Bettmann/CORBIS: 4, 13, 19, 24, 25, 29 (Elizabeth II, Judy Garland, Maria Montessori, Laura Ingalls Wilder); Stock Montage: 9; AP/Wide World: 10, 11 (top), 16, 27; United States Holocaust Memorial Museum: 11 (bottom), 21; Netherlands War Institute: 20, 22; ©Hulton-Deutsch Collection/CORBIS: 23; ©Todd Gipstein/CORBIS: 26; Library of Congress: 29 (Helen Keller); Rick Apitz: back cover

Table of Contents

Captured

August 4, 1944, started as usual for the Frank family and the four other residents of 263 Prinsengracht. The Franks and their friends were Jews, and they had been hiding from the **Nazi** police for more than two years. Their hiding place was a secret apartment behind an office building. During the day, young Anne Frank spoke in whispers to her sister and parents. Everyone tiptoed quietly from room to room, trying to keep their presence a secret from strangers in the office.

That day the group ate their breakfast together. At 10:30, Anne prepared for her daily lessons, taught by her father, Otto Frank. Before they could begin, they heard loud noises coming from the office. Everyone in the apartment froze in fear. Anne could feel her heart pounding wildly in her chest. A moment later, five men stormed into the secret apartment and pointed their guns at Anne and the others. The men ordered them to pack a few belongings. They were under arrest.

The Frank family and four other Jews hid from the Nazi police during World War II. An annex of rooms at the back of an office building served as their hiding place. The office is highlighted in blue, and the annex is yellow.

This photograph of the Franks was taken in 1941, the year before the family went into hiding.

After the Nazi police took away the eight prisoners, other officers rummaged through the secret apartment. They took jewelry, money, and other valuables. One of the officers dumped Anne's diary and writing papers onto the floor.

> *"I see the eight of us in the Annex as if we were a patch of blue sky surrounded by menacing black clouds. The perfectly round spot on which we're standing is still safe, but the clouds are moving in on us."*
>
> —Anne Frank

A friend of the Franks, Miep Gies, gathered up Anne's diary and other papers after the Nazis left. She hid them in a drawer in the office. A few days later, the Nazi police returned and emptied the secret apartment. But Anne's diary was safely put away.

Fleeing Germany

Anneliese Marie Frank was born on June 12, 1929, in Frankfurt am Main, Germany. Her sister, Margot, was three years older. The girls' parents, Otto and Edith, were Jewish. They encouraged their daughters to meet people from many backgrounds.

"We're all searching for happiness; we're all leading lives that are different and yet the same."
—Anne Frank

Otto and Edith Frank married in 1925 and made their home in Frankfurt am Main, Germany. Their first daughter, Margot, was born the next year.

When she was a little girl, Anne liked to make up stories. One of her favorite places to play was the sandbox in the family's garden.

Anne was a playful child who often got into mischief. From an early age, she liked to tell jokes and make up stories. Otto made up stories, too. He told Anne and Margot about two girls named Good Paula and Bad Paula. Good Paula was a well-behaved girl. Bad Paula played with her food, made sour faces at food she disliked, and pulled her sister's hair. Anne later admitted that she had pieces of both Good Paula and Bad Paula inside her.

Otto Frank took this photograph of his wife and daughters while shopping in downtown Frankfurt am Main.

In January 1933, when Anne was 3 years old, Adolf Hitler became the ruler of Germany. Hitler was the leader of the Nazi Party. This political group was **prejudiced** against Jews. Soon after Hitler came to power, the German government began passing anti-Jewish laws. Under the new laws, Jewish people lost their businesses, homes, and freedoms.

Otto believed the laws would become more severe and his family may be hurt. So in the winter of 1933, Anne's family packed up and moved to the Netherlands. This country was **neutral**. It had not taken sides during World War I (1914–1918). For this reason, Otto thought it would be safe from the Germans. The Franks were among 63,000 Jews who left Germany that year.

Nazi Beliefs

Adolf Hitler and other members of the Nazi political party were racists. They believed white Germans—whom they called Aryans—were better than all other people, including Jews, Slavs, blacks, and Roma (Gypsies). The Nazis also thought people who were physically and mentally disabled or who practiced religions they disagreed with should not be allowed to live among Aryans. The Nazis made their beliefs the law in Germany.

Hitler especially hated Jews. In speeches and writings, he told the German people that Jews were lazy and greedy. He blamed them for Germany's hard economic times. Hitler said that Germany could have a bright future if there were no more Jews in the country.

In reality, most Jews in Germany were good citizens. They had jobs as doctors, teachers, lawyers, and business owners. Many Jewish men, including Anne's father, were loyal to their country and had fought for Germany in World War I.

But Hitler needed someone to blame for Germany's troubles. And many people believed him and stood behind him. Hitler rose to power and soon began his plan to gain control over all Jews.

Adolf Hitler greets the crowd at a Nazi rally in 1929. Some people raise an arm in a salute and say "Heil Hitler!" (meaning "Hail Hitler!") to show him their support.

A New Home in Amsterdam

Anne and her friend Hanneli Goslar (right) play hopscotch.

Anne's family moved into an apartment at 37 Merwedeplein in Amsterdam, the capital city of the Netherlands. They liked their new neighborhood and made new friends. Some were other Jews who had fled Germany. Anne's father worked in an office building nearby. He owned a company that sold pectin, an ingredient in fruit jellies.

In 1934, 5-year-old Anne started school. She quickly made many friends. Her best friend, Hanneli Goslar, was also Jewish. Anne was talkative and lively in class. Her teachers nicknamed her "The Chatterbox." Anne studied hard and asked a lot of questions. She especially enjoyed theater class. She liked to imitate people and act out plays. Most of all, Anne wanted to be a writer. She later wrote, "When I write I can shake off all my cares. My sorrow disappears, my spirits are revived! But, and that's a big question, will I ever be able to write something great, will I ever become a journalist or a writer? I hope so, oh I hope so very much …"

In the fall of 1941, Jewish children in the Netherlands learned they would no longer be allowed to go to school with non-Jews. Anne and Margot had to go to a Jewish school that had only Jewish teachers.

Anne's carefree schooldays soon came to an end. By 1939, much of Europe was fighting World War II. On May 10, 1940, the German Army **invaded** the Netherlands. Soon the Germans began passing laws in the Netherlands to separate Jews from other people. Anne and other Jews had to wear a yellow star on their clothing with the word *Jood* (Jew) printed on it. Anne could not ride her bike because the laws forbid it. She was no longer allowed to go ice skating or swimming at the beach. And no Jews were allowed to leave the country. Anne was hurt to see her life changing and her freedom being taken away.

The Germans passed a law on April 29, 1942, saying all Jews had to wear a yellow star on their clothing.

Anne started writing in her diary two days after she received it for her 13th birthday. She filled the pages with her thoughts and feelings. She also pasted in photographs of herself, her family, and her friends.

On her 13th birthday, Anne's father gave her a diary. Her first entry reads, "I hope I will be able to confide everything to you, as I have never been able to confide in anyone, and I hope you will be a great source of comfort and support." Anne named the red plaid diary "Kitty," and it soon became her closest friend.

World War II

When Hitler came to power in the 1930s, the German government began building up its military strength. Hitler wanted to conquer and rule other countries. Japan and Italy also wanted to gain power in the world. On September 1, 1939, German troops invaded Poland. Two days later, Great Britain and France declared war on Germany. World War II had begun.

Every major power in the world fought World War II. Germany joined with Italy and Japan to form the "Axis" powers. They fought against the Allied forces, led by Great Britain, France, the Soviet Union, and the United States.

War raged across much of the world. Germany gained ground in Europe. But in February 1943, the Germans were defeated at Stalingrad in the Soviet Union after a battle that lasted 6 months. Then on June 6, 1944—a date now known as D-Day—the Allies stormed the beach at Normandy, France, and began to drive back the Germans.

The Allies finally defeated Germany in May 1945. But the war continued against Japan in the Pacific region. Japan surrendered in September 1945 after the United States dropped atomic bombs on two Japanese cities. The Allies had won the war.

The Germans bombed these buildings in Amsterdam when they invaded the Netherlands in 1940.

The Franks made their way to Otto's office building. As a Jew, he was no longer allowed to own a business, so he had turned it over to non-Jews who worked for him. The Franks moved into the back part of the building, which was separate from the main offices. Anne called their hiding place the "Secret Annex." A hinged bookcase disguised the entrance to these rooms. Inside the annex, Otto had prepared three bedrooms, a small washroom, a toilet, and a large kitchen. Stairs led up to an attic.

This drawing of the Secret Annex shows the cramped living space that was home to the Frank family for more than two years.

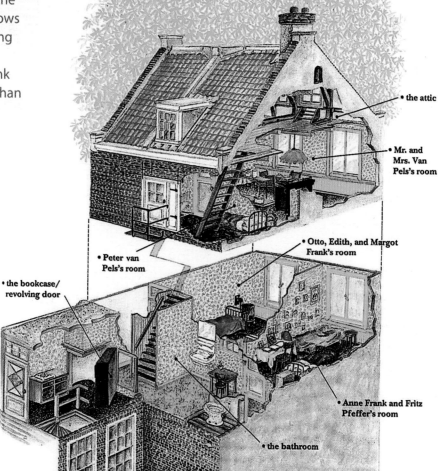

• the attic

• Mr. and Mrs. Van Pels's room

• Otto, Edith, and Margot Frank's room

• Peter van Pels's room

• the bookcase/ revolving door

• Anne Frank and Fritz Pfeffer's room

• the bathroom

Herman and Auguste Van Pels (top) joined the Franks in hiding. They brought their son, 15-year-old Peter (bottom left). Fritz Pfeffer (bottom right) was last to move into the Secret Annex.

Anne quickly made herself at home. She decorated the walls of her bedroom with posters and postcards of film stars. She wrote stories and adventures in her spare time. And she continued to write in her diary. Anne also pasted photographs of herself into her diary and added notes in the margins. Next to one photo she wrote, "This is a photograph of me as I wish I looked all the time. Then I might still have a chance of getting to Hollywood. But at present, I'm afraid, I usually look quite different."

Shortly after the Franks moved in, other Jews who were seeking a hiding place also came to stay in the annex. Hermann and Auguste Van Pels arrived with their son Peter, who was a few years older than Anne. About four months later, a man named Fritz Pfeffer joined the two families in hiding.

Living in such cramped quarters wasn't always easy. The group sometimes argued. Being the youngest, Anne often felt that people picked on her. She wrote in her diary, "I think it's odd that grown-ups quarrel so easily and so often and about such petty matters. . . . I'm the subject of nearly every discussion . . . They criticize everything, and I mean everything, about me: my behavior, my personality, my manners; every inch of me from head to toe and back again, is the subject of gossip and debate."

> *"While others display their heroism in battle or against the Germans, our helpers prove theirs every day by their good spirits and affection."*
>
> —Anne Frank

Miep Gies, one of their helpers who worked in the office, brought the group food and supplies. She put herself in danger every day by helping them. If the Nazis discovered that she was aiding Jews, she could be severely punished. Miep's husband, Jan, and three other office workers—Johannes Kleiman, Victor Kugler, and Bep Voskuijl—also helped the residents of the annex.

The residents of the Secret Annex depended on the office workers in Otto's pectin company to be their helpers. In this photograph, Johannes Kleiman (left) and Victor Kugler stand in the back row. In the front row, Miep Gies (left) and Bep Voskuijl (right) sit on either side of Otto.

The Franks feared the Gestapo would find their hiding place. This Nazi police force helped control countries that were conquered by German soldiers.

While in hiding, Anne missed her friends and schoolmates. She often thought about Hanneli and wondered if she was in a German camp. Hanneli appeared in her dreams. She was thin, dressed in rags, and crying for help. In her diary, Anne wrote, "Is she still alive? What's she doing? ... Hanneli, you're a reminder of what my fate might have been. I keep seeing myself in your place."

The group from the annex kept track of events in the outside world. They heard news from their helpers and often crept into the office at night to listen to the radio. Anne wrote, "Our many Jewish friends and acquaintances are being taken away in droves. The Gestapo [Nazi secret police] is treating them very roughly... We assume that most of them are being murdered. The English radio says they're being gassed."

Although Anne was often upset and worried about the future, she still had hope. She wrote in her diary: "It's a wonder I haven't abandoned all my ideals, they seem so absurd and impractical. Yet I cling to them because I still believe, in spite of everything, that people are truly good at heart."

Betrayed

Anne and the other residents of the Secret Annex lived in hiding for two years and one month. On August 4, 1944, Nazi police officers charged into the annex. Someone had informed the Germans that Jews were hiding at 263 Prinsengracht. To this day, no one knows who revealed the Franks' hiding place to the Nazi police.

For four days, the Franks were kept in a prison in Amsterdam. On August 8, the Nazis transported them by train to the Westerbork **detention camp**, close to the German border. From Westerbork, Anne and her family were sent to Auschwitz-Birkenau, an **extermination camp** in Poland. Unlike other German camps, the Auschwitz-Birkenau camp was built to kill Jews. Some Jews stayed there temporarily and worked as slaves doing hard labor.

After arresting the Franks, the Nazi police sent them to the Westerbork detention camp.

The Franks, along with a thousand other Jewish prisoners, boarded a train like this one. The train took them from Westerbork to the Auschwitz-Birkenau camp in Poland. They rode with about 70 people in a boxcar.

"One day this terrible war will be over. The time will come when we'll be people again and not just Jews!"

—Anne Frank

The train ride to Auschwitz was long and tiring. Anne rode with other passengers in filthy, dark boxcars. Only two small, barred openings let in air and light. There were no seats. Passengers were pressed so tightly against each other that it was difficult to move or sit.

When the family arrived at Auschwitz-Birkenau, the Nazi guards separated the women and the men. It was the last time Anne saw her father. The Nazis ordered the prisoners' heads shaved. This must have been hard for Anne, who was very proud of her long hair. The women were forced into showers and given thin, gray sacks to wear. The Nazis then **tattooed** a number on the left forearm of each prisoner and sent them all to their **barracks**. The barracks were crowded, dirty, and dark.

Women, many with shaved heads, line up outside their barracks at the Auschwitz-Birkenau camp. Anne and Margot were at this camp for only a few weeks before they were taken to the Bergen-Belsen camp in Germany.

On October 6, 1944, Anne and Margot had to say good-bye to their mother. They were transported to the Bergen-Belsen **concentration camp** in Germany, where they would be kept as prisoners. The sisters arrived to the same horrible conditions they had left behind.

Anne soon learned that her friend Hanneli was at Bergen-Belson. Hanneli lived in different barracks, separated by a tall fence. Under cover of darkness, the girls were able to talk through the fence a few times. Anne was losing hope. She cried to Hanneli, "I don't have any parents anymore." The conditions in Anne's barracks were much crueler than in Hanneli's barracks. Anne told Hanneli, "We don't have anything at all to eat here, almost nothing, and we are cold; we don't have any clothes and I've gotten very thin and they've shaved my hair."

Anne and Margot grew weaker and weaker. They became sick with **typhus**. Anne's clothes had become so full of fleas and lice that she had thrown them out. She kept only a blanket wrapped around her for warmth. One day in March 1945, Margot died. Anne died several days later. Hanneli later wrote, "I always think, if Anne had known that her father was still alive, she might have had more strength to survive." Just weeks after Anne died, British soldiers arrived at the Bergen-Belsen camp, and the prisoners were freed.

When the British Army reached the Bergen-Belsen camp on April 15, 1945, they found about 60,000 starving prisoners. These former prisoners line up for soup provided by the British.

A Diary Remains

Otto Frank was the only person from the Secret Annex to survive the German camps. He was freed from Auschwitz-Birkenau by Soviet troops on January 27, 1945. Otto knew his wife had died, but he hoped Anne and Margot were still alive. In June 1945, Otto returned to Amsterdam and soon learned his daughters' fate.

> *"We cannot change what happened anymore. The only thing we can do is to learn from the past and to realize what discrimination and persecution of innocent people means. I believe that it's everyone's responsibility to fight prejudice."*
>
> —Otto Frank

Otto Frank spent the rest of his life sharing the hopes, dreams, and ideals that Anne wrote about in her diary. He died in Switzerland in 1980 at the age of 91.

The Fate of Friends and Helpers

What happened to the Franks' friends and helpers?

- **Miep Gies** tried to rescue her friends from the Nazi police and later served as a witness for an investigation into who betrayed them. She and her husband, **Jan Gies**, had a son. Jan died in 1993 in Amsterdam. Miep wrote a book about Anne and has been honored many times for helping the Franks. She lives in Amsterdam.

- **Johannes Kleiman** was arrested along with the Franks. He was sent to a German work camp and released seven weeks later with the help of the Red Cross. He went back to work and took over the pectin company from Otto Frank in 1952. Kleiman died in Amsterdam in 1959.

Miep Gies risked her life to help hide the Franks. She later wrote a book about the experience titled *Anne Frank Remembered*.

- **Victor Kugler** was also arrested and sent to a German work camp. He escaped several months later and went into hiding until the end of the war. Kugler later moved to Canada and died there in 1981.

- **Bep Voskuijl** left her job at the pectin company after the war. She married and had a family. She died in Amsterdam in 1983.

- Anne's friend **Hanneli Goslar** survived the Bergen-Belsen camp. Her parents dead, she was eventually taken in by a family in Switzerland. In 1947, she moved to Israel, where she became a nurse, married, and had three children. Hannah Pick-Goslar, as she is known today, still lives in Israel.

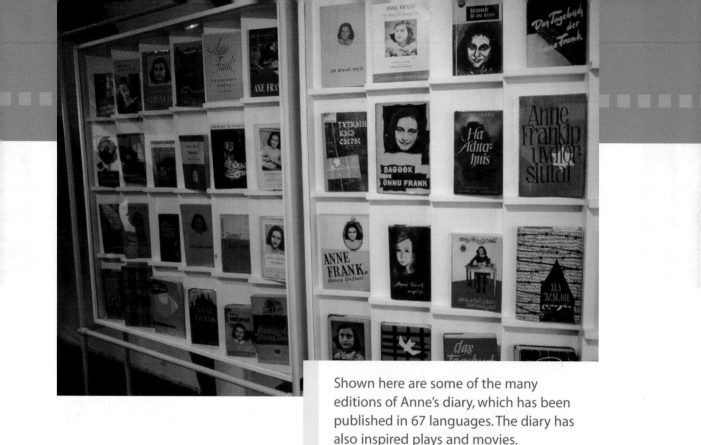

Shown here are some of the many editions of Anne's diary, which has been published in 67 languages. The diary has also inspired plays and movies.

Miep Gies gave Anne's diary and other writings to Otto. He was very moved when he read the diary. He thought the whole world should hear Anne's story. In 1947, Anne's diary was published in Amsterdam, making her dream to be a writer come true. Anne's diary has now been published in 67 languages and is one of the most widely read books in the world.

Otto worked to keep Anne's memory alive. He set up a **foundation** in Anne's name that gives money to schools and religious groups. And in 1960, the foundation opened the Secret Annex to the public as the Anne Frank House. Today, Anne's diary is on display there. More than half a million people visit the Anne Frank House each year to remember Anne and to learn about her life.

Did You Know?

- The Franks were among 25,000 Jews who went into hiding during the German occupation of the Netherlands. It is estimated that at least half of the hidden Jews in the Netherlands were turned in to the Nazi police.

- Some non-Jews were in the "resistance movement." They hid Jews, gave them false documents, and helped them travel out of Nazi-occupied countries. Today, many of these people are remembered and honored as "Righteous Persons."

- The Nazis killed about 6 million Jews—more than two-thirds of all Jews who lived in Europe. This time of killing became known as the Holocaust.

- About 140,000 Jews lived in the Netherlands when Germany invaded the country. Of those people, it is estimated that 107,000 were sent to German camps and 102,000 died in the Holocaust.

- Anne was one of more than 1 million children under the age of 16 who died in the Holocaust.

- Yom Hashoah is an annual day of remembrance for the victims of the Holocaust. In Israel and the United States, it is in the spring. Following the Jewish calendar, Yom Hashoah falls on the 27th day of the month of Nisan, usually in April.

- January 27 is Auschwitz Day in much of Europe, a day set aside to remember those who died in the Holocaust. On this date in 1945, the Auschwitz-Birkenau camp was freed.

On Yom Hashoah in 1998, a crowd gathered for a "March of the Living" through the gate at the Auschwitz concentration camp in Poland. People from all over the world came to remember those who died in the Holocaust.

Important Dates

June 12, 1929: Anne is born.

January 30, 1933: Adolf Hitler becomes the leader of Germany. (age 3)

Winter 1933–1934: The Frank family moves to Amsterdam.

September 1, 1939: Hitler invades Poland; World War II begins. (age 10)

May 1940: Hitler invades the Netherlands; anti-Jewish laws follow.

June 12, 1942: Anne receives her diary as a birthday gift.

July 6, 1942: The Franks go into hiding. (age 13)

June 6, 1944: D-Day; the Allies invade western Europe.

August 4, 1944: Residents of the Secret Annex are betrayed and arrested. (age 15)

August 8, 1944: The Franks are taken to Westerbork camp.

September 3, 1944: The Franks crowd into a deportation train bound for Auschwitz.

October 6, 1944: Anne and Margot are sent to the Bergen-Belsen concentration camp in Germany.

January 6, 1945: Edith Frank dies.

January 27, 1945: Otto Frank is freed from Auschwitz by the Russian Army.

March 1945: Margot and Anne die of typhus within days of each other. (age 15)

May 7, 1945: Germany surrenders.

September 2, 1945: Japan signs a treaty of surrender, bringing World War II to an end.

1947: Anne's diary is published in Amsterdam.

1960: The Anne Frank House opens at 263 Prinsengracht.

August 19, 1980: Otto Frank dies at age 91.

Elizabeth II (1926–)

Three years older than Anne, Elizabeth was born a princess of Great Britain. During World War II, she trained as a second lieutenant in Great Britain's women's services. In 1952, she became Queen Elizabeth II and still holds the crown today.

Judy Garland (1922–1969)

Judy Garland was 16 years old when she starred as Dorothy in the *Wizard of Oz*. The movie hit the big screen in 1939, when Anne was 10 years old. Known for her sweet singing voice, Garland also starred in the films *Meet Me in St. Louis*, *Easter Parade*, and *A Star is Born*.

Helen Keller (1880–1968)

Helen Keller became blind and deaf after a serious illness when she was 1 year old. She overcame her disabilities and became a lecturer and a writer who helped disabled people all over the world live fuller lives. The Nazis did not approve of her or the books she wrote. They burned her books along with the works of other writers in 1933.

Maria Montessori (1870–1952)

Maria Montessori was an Italian doctor and educator. She was the first woman in Italy to earn a medical degree. In 1907, she opened the first Montessori School, which used a new method for educating children. Students learned through activities rather than through lectures by a teacher. Anne went to a Montessori School in Amsterdam.

Laura Ingalls Wilder (1867–1957)

Laura Ingalls Wilder wrote *Little House on the Prairie* and seven other books based on her life as a pioneer girl. She was finishing the last book about the same time that Anne went into hiding.

barrack (BAYR-uhk) a large barn-like building that houses many people; the barracks where Jews lived in concentration camps had narrow bunk beds stacked three high.

concentration camp (kahn-sen-TRAY-shun KAMP) a place where Nazis kept Jews as prisoners; these camps did not have gas chambers to kill Jews, but many prisoners starved to death or died from diseases; there were thousands of such camps in Europe controlled by the Nazis.

detention camp (dih-TEN-shun KAMP) a place where Nazis held Jews until they could be transported to concentration camps or extermination camps

extermination camp (ik-stur-muh-NAY-shun KAMP) a place where Nazis killed Jews, mainly with poison gas in large gas chambers; the Nazis killed more than 3 million Jews at extermination camps; Auschwitz-Birkenau was the largest of six main extermination camps.

foundation (fown-DAY-shun) an organization that raises money to give to worthwhile causes

invade (in-VAYD) to send soldiers into a country to take it over

Nazi (NOT-zee) the German political party led by Adolf Hitler; the Nazi military was known as the SS, and their job was to murder those considered Hitler's enemies, including Jews.

neutral (NOO-truhl) not supportive of either side in a war or an argument

prejudice (PREH-juh-duhs) to judge a person or group of people without knowing the facts; Hitler believed Jews were lazy and greedy people.

tattoo (ta-TOO) to use needles to print on a person's skin; the Nazis tattooed a number on the arm of each prisoner; they used these numbers to keep track of their prisoners.

typhus (TY-fuhs) a disease that is spread by fleas, mites, or lice from one person to another; people who suffer from typhus have a high fever, a severe headache, and a dark red rash; Anne and Margot were among the thousands who died of typhus in concentration camps.

To Learn More

READ THESE BOOKS

Nonfiction

Cooper, Jason. *The U.S. Holocaust Memorial Museum*. Vero Beach, Fla.: Rourke, 2001.

Frank, Anne. *Anne Frank: The Diary of a Young Girl*. New York: Doubleday, 1995.

Lee, Carol Ann. *Anne Frank's Story*. Mahwah, N.J.: Troll, 2002.

Lewis, Brenda Ralph. *The Story of Anne Frank*. New York: DK Publishing, 2001.

Verhoeven, Rian and Ruud van der Rol. *Anne Frank: Beyond the Diary*. New York: Penguin Books, 1993.

Fiction

Drucker, Malka. *Jacob's Rescue: A Holocaust Story*. New York: Bantam/Skylark, 1993.

Lowry, Lois. *Number the Stars*. Boston: Houghton Mifflin, 1989.

Yolen, Jane. *The Devil's Arithmetic*. New York: Puffin Books, 1990.

LOOK UP THESE INTERNET SITES

Anne Frank Center USA

www.annefrank.com

Follow a time line of events from Anne's life, the Holocaust, and World War II; see photos of Anne and read parts of her diary.

Anne Frank House

www.annefrank.nl/ned/default2.html

Click on "English" to see the English-language version of this site. Learn more about Anne, her diary, and the Anne Frank House.

Tolerance 4 Kids

www.geocities.com/tolerance4kids/index.htm

This site gives information about the Holocaust and discusses the dangers of hate and prejudice.

United States Holocaust Memorial Museum

www.ushmm.org/education/forstudents/

Learn more about the Holocaust at this site created just for students.

Internet search key words:

Anne Frank, Holocaust, World War II

Index